What You Can't Have

What You Can't Have

Michael V. Smith

John Barton, Editor

Signature
EDITIONS

Cover design by Doowah Design.
Cover photo by David Ellingsen Photography.
Photo of Michael V. Smith by Daniel Collins.

We acknowledge the support of The Canada Council for the Arts and the Manitoba Arts Council for our publishing program.

This book was printed on Ancient Forest Friendly paper.
Printed and bound in Canada by Marquis Book Printing.

Library and Archives Canada Cataloguing in Publication

Smith, Michael V.
    What you can't have / Michael V. Smith.

Poems.
ISBN 1-897109-09-1

    I. Title.

PS8587.M5636W43 2006   C811'.6   C2006-901264-4

Signature Editions P.O. Box 206, RPO Corydon, Winnipeg, Manitoba, R3M 3S7

for Matt Rader

with thanks

What You Can't Have

I

II Photographs

I

Because the mind will defend anything
it has found the body doing...

— Stephen Dunn

ORIGIN

i

in the middle of silence, the boy
was born, his mother
slowly opening as the hands
of the doctor waited
below her like suitors
patient at the front door

the room grew thin
for that second as
the body first felt air,
the boy spoke
halfway from the womb,
breathless
        his mouth
an open wound, an echo
from that point on

ii

this is the story
never told, people
don't believe a word

could come from a throat
so new and bare, the lungs
like caves unsealed
                    secrets
littering the floor

the newborn
picks a sound, carries it
into the light, the room
no longer filled
                with only
absence

iii

his parents notice
the difference between him
and other children
        how he plays alone
how he forgets more
than he remembers, his eyes
indifferent each time his parents
try to talk to him

they don't know what
to do with a boy
who has only the present,
this first person
without a language

so simple
        he is
was not and never
will be

THE GIRL IS

The girl is a tomb.
You crawl inside her body
and shut the door.

How dark is it
in there, how deep?
with her heart pulsing
in the walls, a great
machine pumping
from distant parts.

She smells of a room
rarely opened to the wind,
to the delicate sun,
she smells of the sea
closed tight
in a child's jar
from the beach.

Come out, little boy,
come out whoever you are.

Climb inside
                my body
and I will birth you
a miracle, like the sky
the sea.

I will give you
my heart, as it pounds
on the beach.

WHAT A MIND CAN MAKE

In a makeshift basement fort, a boy
opened his mouth and took the other
inside him, the dink a stubby
wrinkled thumb bouncing on his tongue.

They counted the seconds then changed
positions, looking for some new way
to fit together. They felt the body's weight
in their minds when it was over,
pulled into the bright sunlight
by a parent's voice calling *Why
don't you boys play outside, it's
beautiful out there.*
      Today, the older boy
works the supermarket training stock
boys to weed out the good fruit
from the bad
     while the younger man
is held fast by the dark
arms of his memory
       by how fresh
his flesh had been as he was shown
what a mind can make,
a body do.

PLEASURE

At the open refrigerator pooling
cool air round their ankles, uninvited
in the neighbour's kitchen,
two boys pick cherries
from a white bowl.

They begin eating two
or three, but fast grow excited
by the sweet taste of getting
up to no good
               until one red globe
remains at the bottom of the bowl
a dark reminder in an
otherwise clean conscience.

The kids pause, surprised
witnesses at their own accident.
As one reaches
for the last juicy bite, his friend
catches him by the wrist.
                     We can't
eat them all, he says.
                 But
we did, the first replies
believing the world
that obvious: I am guilty
or I'm not, hungry or not,
the bowl empty or not

quite, which doesn't matter
when you need to give
your mother a red-handed
explanation.
       *Okay, we'll leave
the last one*, he adds as he plucks
the cherry from the bowl
and holds the flesh
at his friend's
ruby lips.

CARNAL KNOWLEDGE

The boy travels his body
from the inside
                  he travels the ribs
swinging like an ape, caged, or
running loose through the booming jungle of the heart
he traces its spidery vines down the five forks
in the road of his hands,
down his belly, crater to the hipbones,
the gristled pebbles of his toes, he fishes
the kidneys, sails the stomach, crawls
the length of intestinal cave, sleeps
inside the cock's cocoon

all wild and abandoned
he finds nothing of what he's looking for

not even in the twin clouds of his brain
is there a word or sign
explaining
this body of land
body of water
                  with nothing
resembling a man.

AT HIS AGE

The boy stumbles into the dark room
expecting to grab hold of a couch
or table but whatever it was
is gone. He stands still, squinting
to see the outline of something familiar.
It's his grandmother's house. Everyone is asleep.
Here on a weekend visit, he can't help
but walk the rooms, empty in the night.

He wants to shout, but doesn't.
His voice would call the family awake
and fill the rooms, flood his space
with life. He pulls off his pajamas, skin
like soft light wrapped in a sheet, a ghost
in the living room. The boy curls
into his grandfather's armchair
and feels the wool afghan against his back.
He brushes his face into the smell
of cigarette and aftershave, feels their taste
collecting on his tongue.
                          His mind opens.
He is an old man with four children, a pension
and three brothers buried. He is a wife,
a daughter. He is his mother and
his mother's son. How small he sees himself
next to the rest of them,
                          how inevitable.

DISTANCE

The child in the window
seems as thin as his breath
fogging the glass.

The world disappears
with a sigh from his small lungs
as he waits for the mist
to uncloud the street below.

The child is more patient
than the man watching
from the sidewalk
who wants the boy
to hurry up
and wipe the glass.

They are alone together
the boy curled on his windowsill
the man growing cold
outside, his feet damp
from the walk and the freezing snow.

In the next room
a woman is asleep.
She dreams a husband
who wants back in, a boy
so frail these days
she doesn't dare.

DOUBLE

With the heat of his hand and blood
pumping thicker in his cock, the teenager
melts the raspberry ice cube across the pale
body of a girl he met last week.
And though the red juice sliding across her
torso frightens him, he can't help thinking
his lucky tongue gets to lick
her clean before he leaves for his other
lover's house, the too slight
boy from the last row of physics class.

He has no guilt keeping his secret
though soon will have to choose
between the girl's playfulness on city streets,
necking in movie theatres, her
tickled ribs
         and the dark corners or
sullen looks all heavy with intent,
the unavoidable mirror
this young boy's body makes
with his own.

WHAT LOVE INTENDED

Let's be clear: I wanted you
to love me from the start.

You were fine and slender as a boy
at the piano must be.
A doctor's son in our paper
mill town wasn't supposed to have
friends like me with my
department store clothes and blood
shot father, but you did.
                      Six grades and one month-
long kiss later, we were convinced we were
what love intended, we had the front
seat, back seat and rear
of your station wagon, my mother's couch,
your mother's closet,
                       (two winters climbing
through the narrow window
of the cottage where we undressed
one another of family and school
and other selves.
                Weren't we two
people, each day a different story
than by night?
                How much did we invent
to have ourselves more
or less what we wanted
to be
                before we became
five-hour fights with sex in the dark

to forget what needs we couldn't
satisfy?
        When we divided up
our better part of four years, how
could I not love you
even then, half of what I was?

Beginning again, you step out
of the man like second-
hand skin, emerge a woman
I never knew, my ex-boy
friend.
        How do I hold
our past, divided, with you
in your Liverpool home and me
on the far side of the country
you left, single, lonely
as the sky at night when there are
no stars to place us, wondering
if it's true

that we are the people we are,
there is no keeping us together.

ONCE AGAIN

he fucks me like a boy
dry-humping the couch
like I'm poor, or just useless

he fucks me with his tongue
the world hushed and
my heart quiet, he
fucks me as the rain dries,
doggy-style, with my pants down

he fucks me like he never had a wife
and his two kids didn't watch
us flirt in the pool, for a second
he fucks me like a father
fucks a girl

he fucks me the way
my father must have
fucked when he was young
and in love with a woman
who became my mother, if only

if only our too long
detached bodies were
once again making love
like making love could
have once made me.

SEX

you and I
make a third
between us

a child
turned blue
in the womb
he is a lover
we never had

a name
for the past
we whisper

what are we
going to tell him?

secrets kept
like letters
in our inside
coat pockets

the body folded
over and sealed
shut

a mirror touching
its toes, making

itself an image,
the possibility a
possibility

in the middle of sex
he unfolds with a squeal
all hands and fumbling
with our love

we eat his biscuits
stroke his fur
and walk him
thru the neighbourhood
on a collar.

FRATERNAL

How big is the body
I've wanted, brother
what is your size?
                        my tongue
rolls inside the joints
digging
          as an animal
small and determined
to bury itself in the earth
of your flesh
                your bones
and soft body all
bulk and bulge
and flexing weight

as though where you are full
I am waiting
to be filled, pregnant
with your size and shape
with not so much wanting
as wanting to be

I turn sideways
with the night and disappear
in a fold of the sheet
if you won't look at me

look at me, my ribs and curled
shoulders, slim wrists and neck
even my hips curve outwards
handles to the empty bowl
of my belly.

TO DREAM AWAKE

Nighttime in the bedroom, a young man
sees death lying next to him, caressing
the pillow like a lover he'd been waiting for
who never arrived.
                        "Surprised?" the corrupt
figure asks, his fingers running across
the man's cheek to comfort him in a way
only death knows how—who else could be
skinless and yet tender? "Come
hold me a minute."
                        But the man hesitates.
Isn't this the lover's question? A game of trust.
Should he reject death or embrace him,
get on his good side if
indeed he has one?
                        He feels like
a blind man in the near dark,
sees only what happens inches before his eyes.
All he wants is to fall asleep
and forget his visitor until he's alone
again, with any luck, when he wakes up.

To save him the trouble, death yawns
and calls it a night. "Remember me," he whispers,
"I'll find you again," as though they were twins
parted at birth. "Sure," the man thinks, "whatever,"
as he rolls over to bury himself
in soft warm sheets.

II

Photographs

"Elsewhere is a negative mirror. The traveler recognizes the little that is his, discovering the much he has not had and will never have. Italo Calvino. *Invisible Cities.*"

— from the journals of William Gale Gedney

TRUTH

And as the light walks in and lays itself
across the kitchen floor, the countertop
and clutter, does it make the day feel new
or something they've all seen or wished
they'd seen before? Leaning by the far wall
the girls with their square hips, shorts,
bare feet and hair freshly combed,
shirts not pressed, are they girls of today
in their mother's clothes, or their mothers
closer to their age than they realize?

CHANCE

One boot off, foot blistered
from dancing, he stares
at the porch ceiling,
not a betting man, trying
to form the question
he will decide with a toss
of a coin he spent
tonight and got again.

CONFIDENCE

She couldn't brush her hair at the large vanity mirror nailed
above the kitchen sink without a stepstool to see the tips.

Her shirt is sleeveless, her pleated skirt dotted with white.
On the counter rests one spotless jar that makes us love her

slim clean arms in the tin bucket of dishwater, thankful
her hands hold the value of each dish and never let one slip.

PROGRESS

It's obvious, isn't it? Two men talking,
the younger against the hood of the car
isn't going anywhere, turned
to the narrow dirt road behind
the older man who leans out the car
window asking directions (each knows
only where he's been), even
the rearview mirror tilted to show
not the road but his face.

PLAY

One hand raised high to hold
the clothesline and the other
cupping her foot, the girl instructs
her sisters, This is how
the women dance
in their pretty clothes.
On the line: an undershirt,
a dishrag, a diaper.

REST

The girl reclining on the trunk
of the Chevrolet, the trees and the

reflection of the girl on the Chevrolet
and the reflection of the trees, only

the light between them.

OPTIMISM

The car hood is raised
revealing the engine's parts
to the blond baby, freshly bathed,
a man holding her and a man working
on the car, both unknowingly
tanned and full of grease.

WONT

When did the small fair girl at play
on the porch with her toy elephant
last bathe, or
                    what relation
is the teenager
slouched in the worn recliner that
he pays her no mind?
                    He's so busy
having been somewhere
that he's ready to be home
or going again.
                    Whose care
is in the clean jars
and the preserves bottled beside them?
Such attention paid to the boxed
apples no one questions
empty jars will
fill.

LOSSES

Five shirtless men in trousers
idle, watching the oldest kick
the metal guts of a car spilled
between them across the dirt.

SELF-PORTRAIT

There is only a wall, a mirror
and the mirrored room:
used sheets, a fridge, a door, and
a man not unknown to us but un-
recognizable, his head
beyond the frame, the wall
carefully placed.

WISHES

On their spotted
cotton pillowcases
the boys' eyes are licked shut,
each thread of their bedclothes
vies against the other
drawing out their scent—
wood, pine needles, jam
and a mother's cologne.
                    What dreams
can a young boy make while
his brother, asleep
beside him, charges
forward alone?
                    What wishes
can he afford not
to lose?

LONELY

Their mother sits on the porch
so close to their dad in his armchair
he feels the night shift
each time she swings
her hair, tying blue ribbons
at the back. The middle sister
—Sister Three of Five
she calls herself—
helps make two bows.

The air tastes of cool damp grass,
the sun has abandoned the yard.
The children want to stand here,
barefoot on the floorboards,
relaxed, all their skin relaxed
open to the sounds of the woods.

They each would like
to be the one who asks the question
which keeps their parents home tonight,
their father talking
the sun back over the trees.

INTELLECT

She is the dark child who refuses
to wash, who wears the same dress
worn through, her hair pulled
back days later only because her mother
pins it better than she cares. She eats
what she can carry to the woods, sleeps
next to the open window when she's home.
One night her mother woke to her shadow
beyond the door frame, walking away,
her daughter, the girl with ideas.

PROMISE

                The sun joins elbow
blade of grass, grease rag, weathered paint
and 2X4. The boys on the shaggy lawn
wear their white skin like they've never thought
what the day is made for
                                coupled
with their fathers, their fathers' cars,
and the insides of the engines. The men
standing on the lawn figuring
out their day's work or avoiding it
are thirsty, slope-shouldered, soft
in places no one would expect, so sure
they know what they're doing.

★

Even in the far field

there are no tires on the Valiant, weeds
reach the windows, a boy alone

behind the wheel, watching his hands,
has something in mind.

★

Around the bend, two men talk:
the young guy idling in the driver's seat
watches the road and not the fleshy
stump outside his window, the older man
lighting a cigarette with his good hand
catching all the sun of a summer day.

He exhales and returns the lighter,
leans in, says, If you have it shoved
too far up your ass in the womb
you come out like this.

★

See, anyone can try and figure the day
which appears simple.
Thick chest-high grass ends
where the cut lawn
begins.
       But if some
                forgotten deed
has overturned the washtub in the yard,
who can say
how a dark-haired man came to be
barefoot on the shag mat at the edge
of the porch or his neighbour
in a crested work shirt,
hands in his pockets, no belt?

*

In the back lot, between work
and something less than work
six pairs of blue jeans hang on a line,
hold their shape
in the sun and dry.

An old man
scouts beyond the hills of cloud
for another day's weather.

And sex without conversation
sex that's exotic or sleepy…
oh don't let the world tell you
there's a wrong way to have it.

Tell your lovers the world
robs us in so many ways
that a caress is your way
of taking something back.

— Stephen Dunn

SURROGATE

And when I grew up and my arms
were still the two sticks of a boy,
my ribs as sharp as ever, when
my body failed to meet my wishes
like dreams that offer more
than the day delivers, I chose
other men to comfort me.
Each one fit—mouth, ass, hands—
the places where need, salty need
makes pride a thing you swallow.

WHO BROKE MY HEART

James was the sweetest. Not James
the abusive 12-year-old, nor James
of the tattooed knuckles, but wedded
James. James of two kids and wife

in Chicago. Business-trip James. Expense-
account James who bought me all the beer
I could ask for without being asked.
Intuition James. Poppers James. James

who said he never got fucked but wanted
a finger, then more than a finger. (Why is it
all the good fags are married?) Muscle
James, who I couldn't get enough of. James

with the cop's mustache and the salesman's
charm. Big James, the talker. The sweetest,
and I mean this straight up, the sweetest
was how he took off his pants, one ginger

leg exposed, bent over, his hands at the other
cuff, he looks up at me like the thought
of us in a room eight hours from his home
surprised him, boyish James, rabbit-

in-the-headlights James asks me, like he
were making an extra-special request,
"Just don't steal my wallet?" And I say
"Never," like it hadn't crossed my mind.

CHANGE

My bi-lesbo buddy rubs my shoulder then gives
me a shove westward thru the late-night city.
Go, she says. Make us some money. She assures me
she would if she could but the odds for a woman
on the street are higher than she can gamble.
I wonder if she believes men see each other
as equals, but I don't ask. The moment, like the city,
feels bigger than myself, its after-midnight
air carries the heat of my restlessness, summer
sweat convincing my skin it wants more. A couple
boys pace the street. A sporty brown BMW
rolls to a stop. The driver is thirty-something,
his skin grey in the blue lights of the dash.
I say hello; he asks what I do. The tan leather
car seat feels cool right through my clothes.
On his fourth try pulling into the underground
parking spot, I clue in. He's drunk.
So am I. We make out in the car: it reminds me
of being ten and watching *Happy Days*, wishing
I were seventeen so I could go parking
with my boyfriend and it reminds me of being
seventeen with my boyfriend. I quote the price
for a blow job and he shrugs. Let me see it, I say,
meaning the money, but his wallet is empty.
Upstairs, he says, I have cash. Two levels
of penthouse, floor-to-ceiling windows, white
walls. His bed is large as a wrestling ring.
He opens a window flush with the mattress,
a gap I could roll out of, twenty-eight floors
above impact. We have sex and he refuses
to pass out. It ends. I think of only
the cash he still hasn't shown me. Crawling
into the walk-in closet, he drags out a tub
full of coin and counts out my price (which I
don't care to mention) in loonies and toonies.
I walk the morning street, cars racing to work.

I LIKE THE SMALL TOWN, BLUE-COLLAR TYPES

Men like that have it easy, don't they?
Maybe they get down in the dumps, the wife leaves them
then the girlfriend calls it quits, kids show
no respect, dog runs away from home. They lose their jobs,
stop shaving, and go to strip clubs for the only
good time they've had in months.
                              God knows
I'd love to have a wife to leave me, kids to call me names
or a mutt that takes off barking, Find yourself
a new best friend, buddy. I'm outta here.

          Yeah well, I'm not much of a handful
and maybe I got a lot of woman in me—I call her Cookie,
you can too—but tell the truth: Wouldn't
these legs look great extending three
slim feet below the too
short hem of a dress?
                       Picture it: a street corner. Down-
town. Lots of lights. The wind picks up and I grab my shoulders
and rub. Brrr. I'm waiting for any old
vehicle to pull up when a horn
beepbeeps amid the general din of the street.
I turn. The window's down on a 60s blue Chevy, the grille
a mouthful of chrome.
                       Hey little lady, he says and winks like only
he knows how. You don't have to ask twice
before I'm in the front seat kissing
vinyl to my tight ass, 'cause man, he's as close
as I'm gonna get.

SALVATION

If I stood at my open window with
a strange new light falling gold
over my skin now smooth and pale
like cream, no clothes, with breasts
grown full as love, and my cock inverted
to a tight vagina, if my hair grew back
full from the forehead up and fell out
from there on down, if I were a Venus
in the window, all curves, I'd share
everything. I'd masturbate for the men
heading home, the too-tired men
of little hope, the hard workers with
unhappy jobs. They would see me and
cluster on the sidewalk, hats in hand
eyes dewy, a lump in their throats
and pants until someone brave enough
would climb the stairs and find my
door ajar and me, pleased to please.
He would have me on the windowsill
until he was satisfied and each man
from the street, each deserving man
would approach for a taste of this
transformation, so by dawn, I'd be raw
and then, by evening, ready and healed.

HOW I LOVE MY FRIEND!

A midnight adventure above the trees—
three tokes of pot on a wooden platform
anchored in the swaying limbs—so high
we floated on the sea of moonlit leaves.

When the cold crept in our clothes
and snuggled up, we packed the evening
in our pockets and took the few neat steps
down to the plank—five storeys up,
four feet above a peg nailed to
a branch no thicker than my father's leg.
You descended by touch. I lowered myself
off the edge, swung a leg through air
that had never seemed so dark.

I cursed the sky, the trees, the empty night,
the ground I knew was unforgiving;
I swore the best damn words I had
in every fucking order. The minutes
mocked me as I reached with nothing
but the sound of my heart and ten
thousand leaves against the wind.
I stretched again, a man in space,
and still I came up empty.

I'm six-foot-one, I said aloud to right
the night's absurdity, then met
with something solid. Seconds later
I was safely at the base. I thanked
the friend who brought me here.
He smiled, shook his head and said,
I came once with a group of ten and all
the men stayed on the ground.
He could have told me earlier
but I don't care. I made it down.

THE SAD TRUTH

You will only have one drink.
Friends are here toasting your buddy's
sculpture of a worn shoe, xerox-grey,
thick and nearly two-dimensional
which, everyone agrees, is strikingly
simple—common, yet complex—
making you feel you are nothing
out of the ordinary but special
nonetheless. After the first drink
a second can't hurt. The beer is cheap.
You order a third. When your body
begins a real good buzz, your date
taps you on the shoulder. Time to leave.
Across town, you attend another
get-together far more important
than this one—the wine is free.
You fill up on this opportunity
working the crowd of film people
which is your thing or which
you hope to be your thing, except—
here's the disappointing part,
here's what nudges the evening
towards disaster like a small
wind helping a traveller choose
the wrong fork in the road—
you felt better where you came from
than where you have ended up.
You cruise whatever cute men
happen to fall into your line
of vision until who knows
how long later your pal again
persuades you to leave.
Outside, the spring ocean air is
gorgeous in your lungs like dozens
of microscopic fingers pinching
you awake. Sure, you're

drunk. You don't remember
the last hour of the party, but now
you're headed home, walking
through the pooling street lights
on a night all moon and no stars.
You need to pee, excuse yourself
to lurch behind a building and prop
one shoulder against a pine.
You black out only long enough
to find your hand warm
and what you have to admit is gooey
down the back of your pants.
A bad dream, you've shit yourself
and have checked to make sure you did
in fact shit yourself. You wish
you could wake up, night over
only you aren't asleep and your hand
has a very real problem. You remove
your shoes, jeans and underwear but
not your socks. You don't want
to get your feet dirty. Beneath you
the ground is covered with wood chips
and the fallen pine needles are softer
than you expected when you scoop
them up. You wipe your hand,
then your ass. There is comfort
knowing that this isn't so different
really from what it's like to crap
in the woods. You could be camping.
When you're as clean as you can be,
you abandon the Calvin Kleins
that were a gift anyway, pull on
your pants, and then scan
for your shoes which you now
realize you shouldn't have tossed
out of the way without noting
the direction. Again your body
ties a heavy black blindfold

round your mind. You come to.
You aren't at home. You're in the park
with your hands parting the cheeks
of an ass spreading disease
while two feet away another man
pulls at himself just out
of reach with a look that says
he costs more than you're worth.
You lurch to the curb where the old
guy with the big rings you've seen
down here before offers you a ride
in his black Mercedes. The slow
drive home, he doesn't touch you even
once which you hope is more
about respect than with how you
smell. Only in the morning do you
remember the friend you left
on a street corner waiting for you
to pee. Did he walk around
the side of the building and catch you
with your pants down or did he
give up on you as you so often
feared he would, only, this time,
that would be a blessing?

HOMO

Love the body. (Shame about the mind.)

PARTICULARS

A man's two lovers discuss
how they will care for him
before and after he is gone:
meals, bathings, appointments, a full
schedule of repairs and precautions
to keep the body alive, then cremation
burial or a donation to science
if that's still possible.
                                I think he wants
cremation, says the first. *Yes,*
yes I do too, the second replies.
                                Trouble is
they can't solve the puzzle
the ashes pose.
                Who
should keep them, or spread them out?
Where
        should the body go
after the man is gone?

The older partner, the ex
who still calls
his lover home
                won't give him up
a second time, thinking
he never loved me
enough, this guy
got it all.
        And the later lover
regrets arriving on the scene

when the show
is almost over—consider
all he missed and now
will be denied.
                    Even
in the next room, the near-
dead man suffers. *When
can I eat?* he cries, *Won't
somebody change
this fucking diaper?*

DELIVERANCE

After breaking her hip into halves on
the landing, my grandmother lounged
for three days to convince us the couch
was all she needed to return to normal.

Four months later she chose to hide
pneumonia in her bed, determined
she needed neither care, nor water, nor food
to be saved.
        Even on the brightest days
she stood at the door waving hello
or goodbye, unwilling to step outside.

Either the everyday fear held her
to the couch or some other regret
about to happen, her death in a sterile ward,
but only when two officers threatened
to take her to the hospital in their cruiser
did she permit my uncle the injustice
of carrying her to his car.

He leaned over his mother who smelled even
more like herself—sweat, smoke, powder, beer—
slid one arm beneath her back, the other
under her knees, and lifted so slowly, so lightly
you might have thought he could bear just
the best parts and leave the broken ones behind.

DIVIDE

The body dying
opens itself up, splitting
down its centre like
peeled fruit, whole
and ripe, a man
steps out from the skin
wrinkling like a coat
at his feet.

He stands fresh in the darkening
room, his body full
in the dark and the room
full with its windows
open on the city night.

What is to be done, he wonders
running a hand along his brow
for, his lover gone before him,
the man has no comfort,
he has no trust
of each new thing
in the world, the world
made new.
            He folds in half
the bag of his old body
and rolls it up by the feet.
It is twenty minutes to the edge
of the city and the field where
he'd played as a boy. The night

is sharp and clear with
its animal sounds, the road
all gravel and dust.
                    Somewhere
off-centre of the field, with heavens
above him, a bed of cloud,
What thin work it is,
he thinks, this here
and after, as he spreads
the body out, a thin sheet
to cover him.

NIGHTFALL

in memory of Peter McGehee

Picture
        something remembered
you never forgot,
                    a name
so simple
        it defies the truth
a boat drifting round the edge of your mind
old secrets
            bump the sides

If only you knew.

What's inside
this small body?

how much
can it hold?

★

Some time after his death, I found an open and
closed case of a man,
                              so romantic
to be a young writer with my very
own lover I wanted to lose,
                              how romantic

Very.

★

He was my Peter McGehee
he was quick
and he
was beautiful
          his body
missing in the morning—

a writer so good
between the sheets

my bed a book

my lover
my imagination
              :

in the crook of his arm
I would sleep against his skin

each night
we spent
          (our pockets
full of change)
          I cried
oh, if I can arrange the pieces of your
body's puzzle, a model
sealed tight
by your breath
mingled with my own,
                    a gift
to remember you by, to wrap
right around the bones
                    once

and once alone

★

imagine

how pale my morning cheeks, mouth
open to your smooth
white seed   heavy
on my tongue

Hurry, lean forward, I'd say,
and kiss me,
              kiss me
your toothy alphabet

  your once
  red word

Before I wake, remember me this.

★

When did I learn
to love so much
what I can't have?

I won't even ask. I refuse myself
(to ask) who, why, when
will I be happy?

And when will I be happy?

When will this body
be enough?

*

I wanted you to write me, Peter
our correspondence
made letter (by letter)
                    dear
echo,

your lost love sounded
through the dark

sounding the dark
of your loss,
                Love

★

Peter, the craft
blows ashore
with the crying
wind

its open vowel
an open wound

the consonants
absent

it cannot name
what it calls for

and cannot name

★

(I disembark
      unhitch the future

ride bareback
      into the night

you

through this blizzard
drift onto my page, a tender
laden with snow:

patient reader– Is he here yet?

ANSWER THE DARK

Love
is hiding in the shadows
of his body.

His mouth
the shape of my need, and his hands
an invitation, why won't the man
let me find him out?

His bedroom door closed
when I visit, his buttons
all done up save one.
I love too much
what he can't give me

and what little I can get—
what peace. .

Does he too sit in the dark
of himself and ask why
he can't clear the way
to his heart

or am I alone?

How often do the fears I eclipse
inside myself have me venture
forward through diseases
of my lovers long past,
wade naked into pools
of blood turned against itself, or
descend into the knowledge
I will live
too long, with little company.

How can I convince you—
it is not the darkness we can't face
but what it holds

not the light that breaks
but the bulb

not love that fails but the heart
and its capacity.

CHILD-PROOFING

What could we undo? Say
we take away famine, boys bleeding
in the streets, the bullets
fly back into their guns. If we could
refasten the cells of skin and cartilage
that make the tender wound,
each of us furled into the wombs
of our mothers, and our mothers
drawn back, and then again, generations
unborn, to quiet the hungry belly

what would we have to offer
when the tape was all rewound?
There is no sun without its shadow;
no living without consequence.
Let us make the future so unlike its past
we can forget the names of tragic things.

Neela, three weeks new and not
a stitch of language, you're this—
our science fiction. Your tongue
too light for words, two hands
smaller than the Martian
bugs of Mexico.

for Neela Emiliana Rader,
b. November 2005

ACKNOWLEDGEMENTS

At the San Francisco Museum of Modern Art in 2001, I saw a retrospective of William Gale Gedney's black and white photographs. Gedney was an outsider welcomed in by a few dirt-poor families in 1960's Kentucky. Just as his photos are a translation of the living moment into a static record of people in a time and place, I hope the poems in 'Photographs' translate enough of what I saw in Gedney's work to be their own record of what I wanted to share.

I would like to thank the following magazines for publishing some of these poems in earlier versions: *Arc, Descant, Event, Grain, James White Review, The Malahat Review,* and *The New Quarterly.* Thanks to John Barton and Billeh Nickerson for selecting my work for the forthcoming *Seminal, the anthology of Canadian gay male poetry* (Arsenal Pulp Press, 2007). Also thanks to Mosquito Press for my lovely chapbook, *Photographs.* In 2000, "Particulars" won third prize in *Arc's* Poem of the Year contest. "Pleasure" is based on a story Colin Thomas told me about his youth. "How I love my friend!" is a line from an excellent Chris Hutchinson poem, "Disclosure," in *Unfamiliar Weather* (The Muses' Company, 2005).

I would like to thank the other eyes and ears that helped this book be what it is: Liz Bachinsky, Daniel Collins and his writing group, Billeh Nickerson, George McWhirter and my fellow UBC MFA students, and the incomparable Kathryn Mockler. A special thanks to Lorna Crozier (my first love), who went above and beyond, and to Colin Thomas, who helps me with everything. An extra-special thanks to an admirable man, Matt Rader, and to my most excellent editor, John Barton.

I would like to thank the Canada Council for the Arts and the British Columbia Arts Council for their generous assistance over the years.

Thanks to the wonderful filmmaker Nico Stagias, some of these poems have appeared in the video poem sequences *Femme* and *Butch*, available through Video Out Distribution. See www.michaelvsmith.com for details.